Kim and Mag

Written by Caroline Green

Illustrated by James Cottell

Collins

Kim digs

a cap

Kim digs

a cap

Mag sips

sacks

Mag sips

sacks

Kim picks socks

Mag naps

Kim picks socks

Mag naps

15

🐾 Review: After reading 🐾

Use your assessment from hearing the children read to choose any GPCs, words or tricky words that need additional practice.

Read 1: Decoding

- Turn to pages 4 and 5. Ask the children to read the words. Then ask them to point to the animal that begins with the sound /c/ (**Kim**).

- Turn to page 12 and challenge the children to find two words with a different spelling of the sound /c/. (*picks, socks*)

- Turn to page 2 and ask the children read the word **digs**. Then turn to page 6 and ask them to read the word **sips**. Ask them if they can hear the different sounds that the "s" makes.

- Look at pages 14–15 together. Ask the children to name what they see. What can they name from the picture that has a /c/ sound in the word? (*cat, sacks, cap, kite, ketchup, cactus, Kim, clothes, collars, socks, key, book, cup, watering can, skateboard*)

Read 2: Vocabulary

- Go back over the book and discuss the pictures. Encourage children to talk about details that stand out for them. Use a dialogic talk model to expand on their ideas and recast them in full sentences as naturally as possible.

- Work together to expand vocabulary by naming objects in the pictures that children do not know.

- Turn to pages 12 and 13. Ask: Which word means "grabs" or "gets"? (*picks*)

Read 3: Comprehension

- Turn to pages 14 and 15. Ask the children: What is Kim doing? (e.g. *burying the socks*) Where did Kim get the socks? (e.g. *Kim picked them off the clothes line*)

- Ask: Which animal was thirsty in the story? (*Mag*) How do you know? (e.g. *because Mag was sipping*)

- In the story, was it Kim or Mag that was sleepy? (*Mag*) How do you know? (e.g. *because Mag was napping on the fence*).

Collins
BIG CAT

Published by Collins
An imprint of HarperCollins*Publishers*

The News Building
1 London Bridge Street
London SE1 9GF

Macken House,
39/40 Mayor Street Upper,
Dublin 1, DO1 C9W8,
Ireland

© HarperCollins*Publishers* Limited 2022

Wandle Learning Trust name and logo © Wandle Learning Trust

10 9 8 7 6

ISBN 978-0-00-855164-3

British Library Cataloguing-in-Publication Data
A catalogue record for this publication is available from the British Library.

Author: Caroline Green
Reading ideas author: Liz Miles
Illustrator: James Cottell
Publisher: Lizzie Catford
Product manager: Caroline Green
Series editor: Charlotte Raby
Phonics consultant: Catherine Baker
Project manager: Emily Hooton
Content editor: Mollie Schofield
Phonics reviewer: Jacqueline Harris
Copy editor: Sally Byford
Proofreader: Catherine Dakin
Designer: 2Hoots Publishing Services Ltd
Editorial assistants: Daniela Mora Chavarría and Renée Lewis
Production controller: Katharine Willard

This book contains FSC™ certified paper and other controlled sources to ensure responsible forest management.

For more information visit: www.harpercollins.co.uk/green

Developed in collaboration with Little Wandle Letters and Sounds Revised

Printed and bound in the UK using 100% Renewable Electricity at Martins the Printers Ltd.

Get the latest Collins Big Cat news at
collins.co.uk/collinsbigcat

Little Wandle
LETTERS AND
SOUNDS
★★
REVISED
TM

Phase
Set 3

Phonemes covered
/g/ /o/ /c/ c, k, ck

Blending practice

Kim and Mag

Kim digs

ISBN 978-0-00-855164-3

9 780008 551643 >

collins.co.uk/collinsbigcat

A contemporary story

Collins
BIG CAT
Phonics

for Little Wandle
Letters and Sounds Revised

Fox and Dog

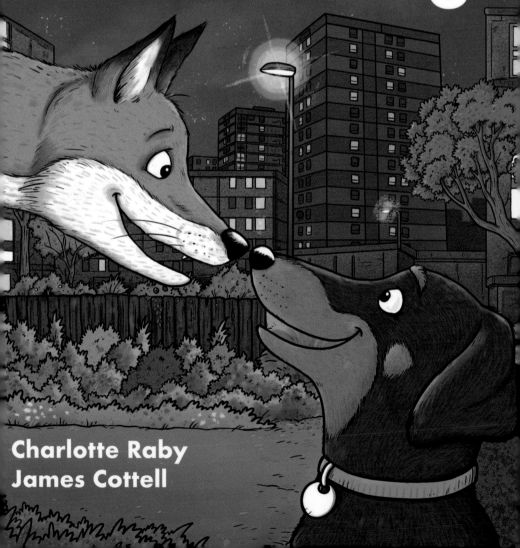

Charlotte Raby
James Cottell

 Before reading

Practising phonics: Phase 2, Set 5
Read the graphemes
- Ask the children to read as you point to the graphemes in any order.

j v w x y z

- Read the tricky words:

and the

How to use this blending practice book
Blend, find and check
- Ask the children to:
  - sound out each word and blend
  - find the image that matches the word or phrase in the picture
  - check their answer by turning the page to see the matching image
  - read the word or phrase again.
- Read the book again, encouraging the children to focus on reading fluently.

Reading at home
This book has been chosen for your child to read at home. They should be able to read it without your help. Listen to your child read. Celebrate their success and talk about the book together. If they can't read a word, read it to them. You can find out more about how to support your child to learn to read at www.LittleWandleLettersAndSounds.org.uk